Praise for

THE
BOOK
OF
ACROSTICS

Let's start with what it all *means*, precisely the place to start. From the start "To the Maestros" filled with recognitions to masters of music, varied kinds of music, and on from there "To be Free" and "The World Around Us" examining the dangerous as well the refreshing to be found all around, the "clues" abound. What is this— "Ephemeron?"

But wait, don't decipher right away, try to avert your glance downward on the page, until all the words are read in a regular fashion, and then assess the coded accompaniment which completes or cajoles, amends or amplifies, makes us think or makes us smile.

The author's skill is paramount. It is not easy to create a puzzle with its answer embedded therein. Clever, yes, but more. There is a reason many have relied on this form of writing; beginning with the Bible, telling those who venture to know, there is more here than meets the eye; found in Medieval literature, the work of Edgar Allan Poe, Lewis Carroll, if you did not know, tells us Alice's real name at the end in this way, if you can find your way *Through the Looking-Glass*. Within *these* pages, "A Small Gift" telling of love, up and down the page. "A Big Pioneer" hinting with "Train colored blue made you a new sensation"—it's all there—for us to find.

~ Howard Richard Debs, finalist and recipient of the 28th annual 2015 Anna Davidson Rosenberg Poetry Awards, and author of *Gallery: A Collection of Pictures and Words*, a 2017 Best Book Awards and 2018 Book Excellence Awards recipient.

THE
BOOK
OF
ACROSTICS

JOHN LAMBREMONT, SR.

TRUTH SERUM PRESS

TRUTH SERUM PRESS

First published as a collection October 2018
All poems copyright © John Lambremont, Sr.

ISBN: 978-1-925536-52-2

Truth Serum Press
32 Meredith Street
Sefton Park   SA   5083
Australia

Email: truthserumpress@live.com.au
Website: https://truthserumpress.net
Truth Serum Press catalogue: https://truthserumpress.net/catalogue/

Cover design by Matt Potter
Original author photograph by Nhu-Y Hau Lambremont

Also available as an eBook
ISBN: 978-1-925536-53-9

Truth Serum Press is a member of the
Bequem Publishing collective

https://www.bequempublishing.com/

This book is dedicated to

the Psalmists and
other Old Testament writers

who initiated the early forms
of acrostic verse.

Also by
John Lambremont, Sr.

Old Blues, New Blues (2018)

The Moment Of Capture (2017)

What It Means To Be A Man
(And Other Poems Of Life And Death) (2014)

Dispelling The Indigo Dream (2013)

Whiskey, Whimsy, & Rhymes (2009)

Preface

I've always liked acrostic poems; they seem to combine Sudoku and the Birnam Wood in verse. The acrostic can serve as a double entendre, an identifier, an expression of feeling, or a witticism. I started writing acrostic poems for mental exercise and to develop my skills in writing metrical and rhyming poetry, and soon became engrossed in the process, finding subjects in nature, music, the seasons, people, and life. Some of the acrostic poems in this compilation are humorous, some are in rhyming couplets, most have rhyme and meter, mainly trochaic and dactylic, and some are free verse. Some are acrostics in combination with other forms, and in each poem in this volume, the acrostic message is spelled out in the first letters of the lines of the poem.

So, you, the reader, have lines to pick up. Have at it, and I hope you enjoy the poems and their acrostic messages.

John Lambremont, Sr.

Contents

To the Maestros

To Be Free

The World Around Us

About People

Calendar Pages

For Practice

Foibles

Of Pens and Poets

Of Body and Soul

To the Maestros

The Sixties were an incredible time in which to grow up. We enjoyed the "British Invasion" of rock-n-rollers, saw rhythm and blues and soul music in America come to full fruition, and watched rock-n-roll become rock. But what I did not appreciate until much later was that the Sixties were also the zenith of post-War modern jazz. These poems are tributes to my music heroes of the Fifties and Sixties (and beyond).

A Big Pioneer

Joyful proclaimer of A Love Supreme;
Oh! How you burned like none ever had dreamed;
Heaven reclaimed you, you passed the baton;
No Giant Steps taken once you were gone.

Chimney sweep tune from a new movie score,
Only you transformed it and made it soar;
Lengthy, bold phrases of mystic oration;
Train colored blue made you a new sensation;
Rivers of Africa murmur your name;
Ascension glory beyond mortal aim;
Never will sheets of sound be heard again;
Eternal blazer, forever you reign.

A Big Idol

Penny Lane so far away, no way you could Get Back;
Apple pie devoured by egg men lined up for a snack;
Uncle Albert begging Admiral Halsey to attack;
Long Haired Lady and her Dear Boy never saw you pack.

Maybe I'm Amazed still at your strange Mull of Kintyre;
crafting Silly Love Songs not always your sole desire;
Can't drive Helen Wheels on a Long and Winding Road;
Awkward end to Helter Skelter that had to implode.
Ram On through your elder years in knighted dignity;
Titled gentry count sheep in the Heart of the Country;
Next time your Band on the Run perfects a new egress,
Eleanor Rigby won't darn your socks nor mend Jet's dress;
Yesterday's excess forced her Revolver to her chest.

A Big Lady

Blues were born into your plaintive voice box;
Infinite time in the school of hard knocks;
Loving the easy life you knew the best;
Lady Day, named by the tenor men's Prez;
Interesting way they arranged your Strange Fruit;
Exquisite style that in our hearts took root.

Home life you longed after time and again,
Only to ride wild on trains with jazz men;
Limited range but such depth of emotion;
In Solitude, you earned our true devotion;
Devils tormented you from east to west;
And while you died a well-chaperoned death,
Yours was the voice we heard above the rest.

A Big Old-Timer

Disney tunes turned into jazz;
Artful player with pizzazz;
Variances in off times;
Effervescent and sublime.

Brought about a campus thing;
Really made the coeds swing;
Unto him Paul said, "Take Five";
Blue Rondo helped both to thrive;
Eugene Wright and Joe Morello
Completed a quartet mellow;
Kept the beat while Desmond soloed.

A Big Mind

Think of One with rare flat-fingered technique;
Hat and Beard gave you a distinct mystique;
Evidence early of genius unique;
Let's Cool One while your sweet glissandos peak.
Off Minor keys pressed with heavy-hand passion;
Nutty tunes composed in bright, Skippy fashion;
I Mean You can't help but feel Bemsha Swing
Under the influence of Rhythm-n-ing;
Suburban Eyes shine in Epistrophy.

Misterioso of space so sublime,
Only you knew 'twas a matter of time;
Nellie in crepuscule first saw the light;
Knew we'd catch on to you 'Round About Midnight.

A Big Lark

Camarillo resident of sly deceptive innocence;
Hardly anybody then that wasn't your constituent;
Altoist magnificent, you circled 'round the floor;
Relaxation made you even better than before;
Lark of Ornithology, the clouds yours to explore;
Infinite in influence, habitually deplored;
Excesses of living left you crashing at death's door.

Prince of post-war players, all the others watched in awe
As your flights soared higher and you soloed without pause;
Reverend of Riff Raff and the King of Keys Perdido,
Ko-Ko still awaits you on the stage at gone Bloomdido;
Even Quasimodo got down once he heard you blow,
Realizing Moose the Mooche was closing out the show.

A Big Icon

Joking sad smoker, warm gun turned on you;
Often you said it would be your just due;
Hold On, Tomorrow Never Knows what's Yer Blues;
No Reply left when the bullets ripped through.

Looking through a Glass Onion did you much;
Every Little Thing she did done double-dutch;
Now Magical Mystery Tour is revealed:
New York the last home for Strawberry Fields;
Only thing left is your Watching the Wheels,
Not A Second Time will we know what you feel.

A Big Vision

Wonder child, you single-handedly preserved a genre;
You deserve all of the recognition thrust upon you;
Never has a jazz man yet received such great acclaim;
Trumpeter, you fast approach Mr. Armstrong's fame;
Only generation left before pure jazz was through;
No one knew it better than did you at twenty-two.

Messenger of music, you direct with style and pace;
Art Blakey could see it, so he put you in his place;
Red Blood on the Fields you wrote of got us all to thinking;
Slave songs in N.Y.C. from the Center named for Lincoln;
All around you spread J Mood, your Citi Movements honed;
Listen to Noo 'Awlins callin' with Levee Low Moans;
It's time you and your kinfolk all made the Jazz Fest scene;
Steepie says he'll treat you to Bayona's on Dauphine.

A Big Iconoclast

Mute man so hoarse with such change in his chords;
In final years, a recluse of few words;
Legacy in making music sound different;
Electric move made him stadium riches;
Steadily sipped he the brew of new bitches.

Dizzy successor in high-fly bird school;
Ably he gave birth to the style called cool;
Varying modes, his bands found Blue in Green;
Imitate? Never, no question mark, clean;
So What if acid was his last new scene?

A Big Significant Other

Gnomes that sat with you knew All Things Must Pass,
Even when Pattie became Eric's lass;
Over time, she found she was For You Blue;
Returned to home to tell you, "I Need You."
Guitar not weeping now, you've run your course;
Equal to your mates, you were the Dark Horse.

Here Comes the Sun, so I Want to Tell You,
Along Blue Jay Way, Piggies cannot fly through;
Realization My Sweet Lord yours, too;
Ragas and sitars could not that undo;
I've Got My Mind Set On You, It's All Too Much;
So Long, Long, Long cigarettes were your crutch;
Old Brown Shoe leather left, your lungs done wrong;
Now you can sing Only a Northern Song.

A Big Star

Classic example of heroin's waste;
Hollywood handsome turned withered prune-face;
Embouchere crushed in a 'Frisco street fight;
Tumbled to death in a Dutch window flight.

Bird from his yard said that you'd be the one
Able to give Miles and Dizzy a run;
King of cool, yes, but a warm crooner, too;
Even when your luck was finally through,
Really was no one that could out-play you.

A Big Clown

Clown sweating upright on many a stage;
Hog Callin' Blues put you into a rage;
Although there were those that said you were strange;
Revered by all for the way you arranged
Love Chants and Folk Forms you sought to attain;
Ecclusiastics you wrought from your pain;
Sorrowful ecstasy, your voice not plain.

Mercurial leader of your small big bands;
Intricate runs from your rough, callused hands;
Nogales to New York was a quick trip;
Growling brown bear of such sardonic quip;
Until this day we have never yet seen
Such a big thumper with long lines so clean.

A Big Red X

Jam-red hot pulsars burn into my ears;
In death, your digits stretch 'way past your years;
Merman in exile, cry cold rainbow tears;
Infinite Axis from which you've no peers.

Heaven and hell, they did both pass you by;
Ever you pondered and still wondered why;
Never together, you weren't satisfied;
Dry stone not knowing sweet Mother Earth's eye;
Rise up like Jesus, show Elvis, show John;
Initiate us in the great beyond;
X-Man we treasured, so wasted, so gone.

A Big Seeker

St. Thomas more to us than just your place of origin;
Oleo and Doxy gave the man in green a grin;
New sounds found in Tenor Madness gave us new insights;
Near to heaven with Blue 7's bright lights borne by night;
Yet, we get the sense that Airegin is not spelled right.

'Round the globe you traveled to seek culture and the truth,
Only to return home to invent yourself anew;
Leader of a trio when you blazed trails Way Out West;
Legions of jazz tenor men swear you're their very best;
Infinite in influence, inventor of the stroll,
Never resting on your success, always playing bold,
Saxophone Colossus, may you long stay on your roll.

A Big Underdog

Richard was your name at birth, but few recall that now;
In an Octopus' Garden, singing was allowed;
No No Song made you strong, so don't Back Off, Boogaloo;
Good Night to your Photograph is what I say to you;
Obviously better than the Best, your time kept true.

Starkey still your surname, but you shortened it a bit;
Tried to do some movie roles, and you were a good fit;
Act Naturally, they said, and you thus bagged Barbara B;
Rock on with your All-Starr band deep into this century;
Really underrated, but still held in great esteem.

A Big Messenger

Rastaman Vibrations you sent bounded 'round the world,
Only to return to the nest of Three Little Birds;
Being of One Love was one thing to which you aspired,
Everyone knew Slave Drivers would quickly Catch A Fire;
Rastafari you spread with your Roots, Rock, and Reggae;
Taught you how to wield a Small Axe in a bigger way.

Never let believers down despite some desperate days;
Ever-faithful to your Jah whom you gave thanks and praise;
So Much Trouble In The World you had to declare War;
Told us of a Natural Mystic that would conquer all;
All the music that you made made you a world-wide star.

Man Forever Loving Jah until his dying day;
Africa Unite tonight and for his visions pray;
Redemption Song a sentiment that lives in us today;
Leader of a revolution in a Jammin' way;
Easy Skanking Rebel Music is his legacy;
Yes, just Who The Cap Fit is still clear to those who see.

To Be Free

Most of the poems in this volume are rhyming and metered, but this is by accident, not by design. There is no rule that says acrostic poems can't be in free verse, and I do not believe in rules for poetry, save formal poems. Here are some free-verse acrostics.

A Big Bog

Sun hurls hatred through green boughs;
Water lilies higher than hip boots;
Able to move naught below;
Muck, barely half-solid, yields;
Peregrine eyes circle high;
Exhaustion and near-certain
Drowning awaits.

Football Hero 1967

An aged yellow photo shows a taciturn smile, the young
Reserve officer in full dress. A Rotary magnet
Still clutches and will never let go, gone

Laughter still audible in the kitchen, and
Only I stand in the heat, alone, his family flown years
Now. I think of the glory days before the Boy
Genie escaped through the dropper and into his vessel
Arm; yes, before his time in Viet-Nam.

Victories healed his broken bones, his grace shown on
Inside carries on the belly dive, but his
Trophies were boxed like bed springs, past honors
All packed up and hauled away. His folks had

Been told of Dong Ngai jungle fever, but didn't get the
Real story about the Tet Tetanus Shot and his
Evening death in a Hue hospital.
Veterans Affairs closed his file quickly, and
Issued an oblique communiqué, but I knew
Sure as rain the Junk Man took him away.

A Late Breakthrough

Later, the cheese melts we abandon to
Omnipresent ants. Mark high the
Sun, set course for the swamp
Through a tall bamboo thicket that

Inside is an anti-forest, green khaki canopy
Nearly blots out all light. Stalk-surrounded, we

Tiptoe along, and within quiet minutes we
Have become confused; lush summer exudates a heat
Envelope to drown us like bagged pups.

Concentric paths we traverse, humbled,
Angry blame thrown as we pass marks that re-appear.
Now worry turns to panic; we thrash
Empty-handed through the yellow maze, fight to

Break through verdant mirrors to a door unknown,
Reaching for a exit handle not there, not
Able to find the hole at end of the fecund
Kaleidoscope. In smothers of anguish
Extreme, we stumble dumbly out into pasture dusk, saved.

A Far Cry

Nexus of fire-breathing locusts;

Ignition by transmission from the finned console;

Groaned confession of a willing transgressor;

Harbinger of prophecy by the righteous;

Transferred flesh in deposits certain;

Mark of no random visionary.

Arcane verses in cursed support;

Reap the teeming celluloid mass,

Envelope the remains, and repeat.

Little Evie

One spring night, after birthday cake and candles,
Under a beaming moon, I sat on a garden bench,
Resting, a little Vietnamese girl at my side.

Feyly playing her hand, she said, "I'm bored, Uncle John,
And my mom says we have to leave soon.
Tell me another story." I asked her
Had she heard of Johnny Watermelonseed.
"Everyone knows that one! He planted
Red apple trees everywhere!"

When I pointed out her error,
Her chagrin at first showed, but at
Once she bounced back with a petulant, "Tell me."

And so I began to tell a tall tale,
Relating the myth of the troublesome
Tyke that always swallowed the melons' seeds.

In moments her eyes grew wide with wonder;
Not once did she disbelieve.

Her head nodded slowly as I described
Ear and nose passages sprouting and growing,
And later, ripe watermelons dragging on the ground.
Very quickly, she began to interrupt me at the
End of each segment with a comment
Never-failing, "And then he died!"

Hastily, I assured her that the surgery had saved him,
And then she grew quiet and somber.
Lowly, she murmured, "I saw a dead bird; a million
Little ants were eating it." I made the old
Observation that all living things must die, and I
Watched her young face grow sad.
"Even you, Uncle John? But I don't want you to
Die." I tried to explain about Heaven,

But she had too many questions,
Even asking if ants get into coffins.

Telling her of togetherness in the hereafter,
Her solemnity slowly dissolved. Said she, smiling,
"Yes, I understand."

Next, we heard her mother calling,
And time for our good-bye; she left me with a
Mirthful aside over her shoulder:
"Everyone's going to die but me!"

A Big Tiger

Lately, I've watched a black and yellow butterfly
Ease its way around the patio plants;
Pretty thing, a tiger swallowtail;
It brought back childhood collecting trips with
Dad and his colleagues in the vast Kisatchie,
Only I still on the hunt at dusk,
Proud capturer of trophy specimens, my
Tiger then a state record size,
Even now on permanent display.
Recently, I submitted for The Butterfly Issue,
Although my subject was a Luna moth; the
Editor that rejected me must know entomology.

Saturday Free Concert

Playing live, piano master of
Rhythm and time, a mentor to jazzmen,
Of a kind of his own;
Fingers ebony chopsticks in harmony,
Exact beat with each succeeding measure,
Soulfully warbles his songs of New Orleans;
Sunglasses raised high to the heavens;
Oblivious to us, his neophyte listeners;
Rocking us in our homes.

Legend little known, digits splay sweet madness;
Obliging gifts to ears uninitiated;
Never within safe classification;
Genius unsophisticated, beyond decades;
Hardly looks down to the keys;
Ably mesmerizes dumb college kids;
Impish winks, white haired smile; we
Rush the platform to shake his hand.

The World
Around Us

There is no better source for poems than nature. Poetry is all around you, just look for it!

Black-Eyed Susans

Wastrels reside on the side of the road,
Idyllic in their indifference;
Lifting their palms up for alms unknown,
Do nothing to earn their sustenance;
Finery of color in bright-patterned clothes,
Long standing and mostly unnoticed;
Owners of naught but a lone patch of ground,
Wave beckons at all our approaches;
Ever beyond our reckoning, and
Reckless in their livery, they
Smile as we drive quickly by.

Of Corpse

Dead body rests in my back yard,
Only the parasites grow;
Wonder who chopped off the feet and arms,
Now the veins are exposed;
Early dismissal from a life so hard;
Disposal is needed, I know.

Try to bring myself to it:
Retreat to remembrances kind;
Efforts I take can't renew it,
Effortless death on my mind.

A Big Struggle

Earthworm wriggles on the peaty loam
Underneath the noon sun's deadly burn,
Trying blind to find its earthy home,
Helplessly twisting, desperate to return;
Almost gone now, emitting thin foam.
Now I wonder if it's death it yearns,
And a strange feeling creeps through my bones:
Stamp out misery, as it is the worm's turn?
It finds a break in the soil of the urn,
And quickly disappears, as do my concerns.

A Big Dalliance

A curious hummingbird darts and hovers,
Mesmerized by the harlot bloom;
Aromas draw him slowly nearer,
Red petal cup serene and seductive,
Yellow pistils thrusting saucily.
Longing overcomes the excited suitor, his
Lingering kiss met with an airy appraisal;
In moments, he sets a course and is gone, to
Share a sweet tale with his brothers.

At Sundown

Cathedral bells call them from their high places of rest,
Hidden all day in their lofty quiet nests;
Into the evening city sky they quickly pour,
Marking well the time of the twilight cocktail hour;
Now in swarms of flight, high above the street they soar;
Each flies alone while it skips and darts at random;
Yet, their spiral aerobatics always turn in tandem.

Silly feathered chirpers of the golden dying light,
Watching your ballet ends every day exactly right;
I wonder very often how you never once collide;
From my third-floor window I can see you eye-to-eye;
Today now gone away in your dusky rite of passage,
Sunset come tomorrow entertain me with your masses.

Red on Green

Crested explorer makes his landing,
Assesses chances in the field of green;
Readily seen through my correction,
Despite the safe distance between;
I spy his red cloak, his nose pointed;
Now his black eye turns to me,
As he searches in the branches,
Looking for young figs to steal.

The Caretaker

Brother B cares for his sad saffron ladies,
Under his spell, they give him all that they've made; he
Muzzles his love into each golden ear,
Bread money taken for their musky labors,
Lip service given to their vain complaints.
Each encounter ends with a silky whispered threat, as his
Blazer's sulfur sash boldly signifies his tribe, and
Even though he has another bouquet across town,
Early in the evening, once again, he'll make his rounds.

Ephemeron

Young are you, ne'er to grow old;
Esperanza dances with a gait so bold;
Lively skips as your limbs unfold;
Life long over before the leaves turn gold;
Opulent body that no one can hold;
Wanderlust seems to be your only goal.

Beautiful moment in a barrel roll;
Undulate gaily as you stir my soul;
Tantalize daily with a tale untold;
Tempt me fleetingly to break your mold;
Evanescent breezes lift you up whole;
Roses below look up to scold;
Far away from me is where you'll go;
Last look back for me to behold;
You are gone now, and now I feel old.

About People

These poems range from humanity in general to specific persons. Eddie Anderson was a dear friend and colleague who we lost to cancer. I wrote poems to cheer him, and later the epitaph. The Laramore poems were commissioned by another close friend to commemorate the graduation from high school of her children; payment consisted of two lunches.

Quality People Wanted

Quiet, wan smiles are their sad invitation,
Usual ethnic diversification;
Almost hypnotic in staid reverie,
Lulling me into a state of well-being;
I find myself staring, and I don't know why;
Terrible thirst for some Canada Dry;
Yet, Newport cigarettes are all I buy.

Pause at the counter, look over my shoulder;
Each sends encouragement just to be bolder;
Obvious move is to ask the cashier,
"Please, can I be a new applicant here?"
Let me list for you my qualifications;
Ever will I take the worst degradations.

Worries surround me; I'm sure to regret it,
As I can't separate debit from credit;
Never in this life could I do this job;
Try to forget it, it shouldn't be hard;
Exit now, quickly, the door is this way;
Death to a life at the damned Circle K!

Major Thoroughfare

Airport route taken to old New Orleans;
Interstate highways were still but a dream;
Restaurants' rich luxuries making the scene;
Lights of the motor hotels brightly gleamed;
Innocent child took in all he could see,
Neon in flashes of pink, blue, and green;
Everything modern and everything clean.

Havens for homeless folks now there abound;
Ignorance, poverty, filth all around;
Ghetto home dwellers in houses run down;
Hospital's charity cannot be found;
Wandering hookers in dirty silk gowns;
Armed doped-up dealers sell drugs by the pound;
Yes, this was once a real swell part of town.

A Big Country

Land of the freak and the home of depraved,
Inbred with cousins from cradle to grave;
Vicious attack dogs kept as family pets;
Isn't a safe place for blacks to live yet;
Nary a mouth that contains all its teeth;
Go to hell if you don't share their beliefs;
Stoned redneck hippies that try to shine bucks;
Traveling meth labs on backs of old trucks;
Only place where Wal-Mart's the best around;
New Bass Pro Shop is the talk of the town.

People keep moving there; I think they're fools;
Argument is they have much better schools;
Ruining the jury pool long since begun,
It's infiltrated by Republicans;
Some people there long for the good old days;
Hot, burning crosses of the K.K.K.

A Big Sac-au-Lait

Listen: ever wonder why,
Almost no exceptions,
Children of all cultures cry
To Mother with an "m" word?
Asians call their mothers "ma,"
To French kids, it's their "mere."
I've heard "madre" and "mama,"
Old Romans said "mater," a
Need that started somme-where...

A Big Extraction

When will it all end? You may want to know;
Is it the same way it was years ago?
Sons and daughters will depend on you still,
Dad's recompense and Mom's mad cooking skills;
Over and over they will turn to you;
Maybe it's just what you want them to do.

Time was a child turned adult at eighteen,
Or was it twenty-one, or when married?
Only just yesterday they were newborns;
Time slipped away as they took on new forms;
Happy the days when they come to your home.

Remember this: they will always be yours,
Eating your vittles, regaling your snores;
Making their mom mad occasionally,
Only to win her back with a small, "Please?"
Very much grown, perhaps not full adult;
Able to volley your teasing insults;
Love them forever, whatever results.

Birthday Lunch

Hearty meal this day which we've just ingested;
Acme for seafood, as you had requested;
Plump, juicy oysters prepared several ways;
Perfect repast for a warm March mid-day;
Yet, there was one under catfish's sway.

Brother in arms, but a friend to all states;
Invites us annually to celebrate;
River of life upon which we all drift;
Today we gather to give him a gift.
Hoping this gift is not given too late;
Didn't remember that this was the date;
Always you've tried so to give us a lift;
Yet, there were times when you needed a spliff.

Enjoy your day, dear sweet brother of mine;
Do not forget me when it is my time.

A Long Time

'Twas long ago, if you measure the time,
When Eddie took Janet and said, "Please be mine."
Even then Rachel a gleam in his eye;
Newly-weds learning a love so sublime;
Telling themselves how to complete their heaven;
"Yes!" Eddie yelled when they had their son, Evan.

Families grow quickly, and so this one did;
Intellect passed down from parents to kids;
Very close-knit, with a sense of direction;
Everyone knew they'd made the right selection.

Yesterday's vows they today will repeat,
Evan and Rachel in their front-row seats;
Able to see Mom and Dad still in love,
Reveling in what God gives from above,
Sending it down on the Wings of a Dove.

To Our Young Graduate

Second name the same as flowers that always smell sweet;
A's and B's the norm for you, high school now complete.
Mustang, we know, wasn't quite your ideal choice of car;
Admit now that little ponies do take good girls far.
Now it's time for you to change your University,
Trying to decide how you will seek sorority;
Happiness will follow you throughout your college days,
And we know your success will continue to amaze.

Rising high above the rest is nothing new to you,
Or you might delight us with a brand-new dig or two;
Strive to maximize your strength in spirit and in mind;
Education is one thing that no one leaves behind.

Languish at the Lagoon every afternoon you can;
And in the Bahamas, you will soon perfect your tan;
Return ready for the challenges the fall will pose,
Adamant that college girls do not wear high school clothes.
Maybe we'll convince you that new shoes will set the tone;
Only thing you'll lack, perhaps, is a matching I-phone;
Rest assured we love you so, and back you all the way;
Every day with you, dear daughter, is a blessed day.

Landon Sean Laramore

Lad no more, you're on the eve of your eighteenth birthday,
And you'll go to college at a school just up the way;
Now we hear you're aiming for the Tigers' Golden Band;
Don your hat and blow your trombone across Dixieland!
Only one reminder as you travel near and far,
Next best friend to trombone is your very own guitar.

Show us how you make those robots pivot, pause, and run,
Even though your engineering's only just begun;
Ample time ahead for you to finish your degree;
Now you must pursue it with devout sincerity.

Leave a bit of time to have some fun with on-line games,
And do not let Internet trolls give you any blame;
Relish in the thought of how successful you will be
After you have finished school and become a P.E.
Make new friends as you attend our university;
Once you get there, you will see complete diversity;
Remember us in all your days as new worlds you explore,
Even take us fishing if it's not too much a chore.

Eddie Anderson
in memoriam

Earnest in demeanor and diminutive in size;
Death did not once daunt him, a true hero in our eyes;
Did his best to live his life in calm and genteel style
In his work and in the woods; in both, he traveled miles;
Even now, we see his face and miss his gentle smile.

Allstate was his client, but to do right his concern;
Never did he break his word or do an untoward turn;
Diplomatic in his choice of words, and always kind;
Educated past the law, an intellectual mind.
"Rest in peace, dear brother, you are not forgotten here;
Sadness can't dispel in us good times we shared for years;
Of our friends, you were the one whose faith was ever strong;
Now you are in Heaven, which is just where you belong."

Our Father

Eighty hasn't slowed him down, still cooking up the chow;
Dining club's best elder chef, whether it's fish or fowl;
Wielding at some stray weeds that formidable eyebrow,
Able to converse on-line as his time will allow;
Really had forgotten all the "Woo!" and the "Pow! Pow!"
Doing what he likes to do, nothing to stop him now;

Now I lift my glass to him, and hope I've made him proud,
Even though there are times when he says I am too loud;
Legacy of lawyering, but scientist his trade;
Sons he had but one, and I am glad to bear his name;
Opportunities he gave me I put to good use;
Never did he let me slough off or make an excuse.

Lepidopterist by trade and leader of Reserves;

Army in Korea, field artillery he served;

Made a reputation with the lipids he observed;

Became quite acquainted with a ray's decaying curve;

Raised four normal children, with his family name preserved;

Educated generations, acclaim he deserved;

May have been the longest member of the PTA,

Only golf has passed him, but there's still the PGA;

Now the U.S. Open closes out on Father's Day;

Try to call him when it's over, he'll have more to say.

Calendar Pages

Over the years, I wrote acrostic poems to share with family and friends to celebrate holidays and special days. Here they are presented in chronological order.

A Big Shadow

Gray blankets my horizon;
Rain drowned my smile.
Out in the cold wet,
Under the willows,
Never gone for long,
Death is an umbral neighbor;
He hovers at the gate,
Ogles a hole in the dirt, and
Gabs gobs about weather.

Dry my weeping eyes,
Although no sun shines;
Yard Rat promises better.

A Valentine's Day Poem

Angels sang the day we met:

Velvet voices filled my ear
As you swept by, so near and dear;
Loveliest maiden I'd seen yet,
Enticing eyes and a lively step.
Never knew exactly why
'Twas the time that I said "Hi";
In the way, our race and tongue;
Never thought what we'd begun
Even now would keep us one,
Same as when we were so young.

Dearest one, you've made me whole;
Always love me, heart and soul;
Years from now, when we've grown old;
Still you'll be the one I hold.

Please know this: for all my life,
Only you will be my wife;
Ever will our love bells ring,
Making those sweet angels sing.

A Big Double Holiday

Hearts and flowers aren't the only things today, my dears;
Always seems there is more than to what the eye appears;
Prayers are due to ancestors that went before us here;
Peaceful thoughts go to them, so try to hold back the tears;
Yes, it is the time that comes one time this time of year.

Char the pig on open coals and savor the best slice;
Have a piece with skin attached, the flavor's very nice;
Itsies run around and wave red money envelopes,
New bills folded for good luck are carefully enclosed;
Elders sit on lawn chairs and exchange their fondest hopes;
Sisters supervise the games, and teach the kids the ropes;
Everyone is happy, as this holiday's the most.

Now the sun is setting, and I slip out for a smoke;
Evening is beautiful, although it is still cold;
Wishing I could wait here for the rising moon of gold.

Yelps are coming from the house as fireworks begin;
Even longer strings of poppers than I've ever seen;
All are cheering as we chase the bad spirits away;
Really is the best way to enjoy this joyful day.

A Big Prelude

Ladies and gents from all over the world
Undulate weight in their Mardi Gras pearls;
Never knew better than that other name:
Day before Tuesday's but more of the same;
It's the penultimate, so have no shame.

Go see King Zulu shake hands with King Rex;
Revel in bosoms of the fairer sex;
All bets are off until your belly's full;
Safe 'til Ash Wednesday, keep dancing, you fool.

A Big Fibonacci

Fear

Ides

Before

Old March days,

Now Fat Tuesday plays;

Ascends King Rex, mirth incarnate;

Captains and couriers of his Krewe toss down doubloons;

Costumed revelers crowd the streets for throws, drink
steadily flows, wild hi-jinks in scanty clothes;

In the morrow, not much sorrow; Lent descends, must
make amends, try to stir your sleeping friends;
streets are swept, piled-up neglect, best Mardi
Gras yet.

A Big Forbearance

Lesson learned at the Master's feet:
Eat not when one should not eat.
Now it's time; all must repent;
Time for fasting, time well-spent.

A Big Party

Summer is not here yet, and they must have a release,
Playing music so loud locals call out the police;
Roving hordes of males are trawling up and down the beach,
Interested in netting any easy girls in reach;
Never stop their drinking, it's oblivion they seek;
God protect them, as it's going to be a crazy week.

Boys will always be boys, and it's certain they'll chase girls;
Red, blonde, or brown hair, straight-haired or with curls;
Education set aside for ice chests full of beer,
And when people point at them, they bray, howl, and jeer,
Knowing that they rule the beach for one week every year.

A Big Good-Day

God sent us His only Son,
One to show us all The Way;
Only one way to His Heaven,
Do you know to Whom to pray?

Forget not His suffering;
Roll away the massive stone;
In death, He redeemed our sins;
Dying so, He made us whole;
And soon we will be rejoicing;
Yes, once more, He'll save our souls.

A Big Sunday

Haven't had this kind of two-some before,
As we're without kids on Masters' Sunday;
Putters and drivers are proving a bore;
Perhaps Amen Corner won't come by my way,
Yesterday's clouds may send downpours today.

Every year golf balls fly just a bit faster,
As younger swingers seek jackets of green;
Sometimes, contenders find a wet disaster;
Time was, we cared more for a different scene;
Everyone should know there's just one true Master,
Rising up from the dead, our souls made clean.

A Big Easter Bunny

Each child within us wants a chocolate rabbit
As the highlight of his own Easter basket;
Sitting up top in a decorative box,
Tall in the ears, and of one solid block;
Eyes made of candy so sweet to the tooth;
Rising high from the nest, calm and aloof;

But, by the afternoon, his ears are gone;
Under duress, the eyes see what's been done;
Next goes the head, then the torso and feet;
Now it's good-night, as engorgement's compete;
Young kids and old goats both crave this rare treat.

On This Day

Consider the boulder that had to be rolled;
Hardly a trifle, the weight of our souls;
Realization of what He'd begun,
Infinite kingdom from God's only Son;
Saving us from ourselves on this, His day;
Taking us Home when we have lost our way.

Hand of the Father revealed in His plan,
As He gives witness to immortal man,
Showing us Life past our deaths once again.

Reach deep within yourself, look at your heart;
If it is empty, make this day your start;
Seek out the answers that He can provide,
Even when faith cannot hold back the tide,
Never forget He is still at your side.

A Big Fiesta

Now come the best two week-ends of our year;
Everyone's sipping on cold drinks and beer;
Wynton Marsalis' orchestra's here.

Open-air stages, immense canvas tents;
Roots, rock, and heritage, time so well spent;
Look at your schedule and map out your day;
Exultant Nevilles sing, "Hey Pocky Way,"
And while the Gospel Tent rolls in full sway,
Neil Young gets tuned up and ready to play;
Second-line with a brass band, and sashay.

Join in the fun and forget all your cares,
As music styles slide on by through the air;
Zoo of humanity moves everywhere;
Zebra-masked dancers hip-shake Congo Square.

Fairground food vendors all plying their wares;
Extra hot sauce is right there, if you dare;
Spread out your blanket and enjoy the fare;
Try to remember to bring your camp chairs.
In the warmth you bask, yet everyone's cool;
Various things for the kiddies to do;
And as the sun sets in red and blue hues,
Look toward tomorrow, Badu and U2!

To My Other Mother

Had I my life to live again,
All that I know is this:
Passion would still find me when,
Perchance, your lips I'd kiss;
Your love has been pure bliss.

Many times I've thought about
Our life, and how it's been;
Togetherness year in and out,
Heartfelt love 'til the end;
Every time we did without
Restored our faith, my friend,
Since our love always mends.

Dearest one, just let me tell you,
All my love is yours;
Yes, today and toujours.

A Small Gift

It is now your birthday, so here's what I'd like to say:

Lady, you're still lovely, even with a touch of gray;
Only you could love me and my most peculiar ways;
Very much a part of me until my dying day;
Even then, we'll be together in heaven always.

You are the love of my life, you've made my life complete;
Our life as husband and wife has always been so sweet;
Underneath the stars tonight, our kiss will be our treat.

To Dad

Hardly a day passes that I don't remember when
All of us were family watching T.V. in the den;
Past times are over now, as we've gone our separate ways;
Perhaps we've been closer; yet, there's something left to say:
You are still the one that gets our thanks on this, your day.

Failure not an option when you sent us off to school;
Able to split our sides when you played the zany fool;
Teacher of appreciation of good wine and food;
Have to say, among the dads, you were the coolest dude;
Even though, of your kids, I know I am not the best;
Really, I resemble you much more than all the rest;
Sorry now for all the times I put you to the test.

Dad, this poem's to thank you for all the things you've done,
And to let you know that I am still my father's son;
Years from now, I'll still be working on what you've begun.

A Big Anniversary

Another year we've been together;
Never have I loved you more;
Newlyweds at heart forever
In all climes and on all shores;
Verses I shall write you ever;
Ever to you I implore:
Raise my life up, make me better,
So much better than before;
Always my love exceeds letters,
Reaching new heights as it soars;
You, my love, I do adore.

Our Anniversary

Once a year, we celebrate this very special day,
Understanding how it was we came to be this way,
Rejoicing together that this way we'll always stay;

And as I look back upon these thirty-six past years,
Now I see more clearly why our joy was mixed with tears;
Never worry, lessons that I've learned I will keep dear.
It is not a marvel our love's stood the tests of time,
Vanities were set aside so our hearts could entwine;
Even now, we learn how to make our love more divine;
Revelations come each day both to heart and to mind;
So, as we turn this page together, this I say to you:
All Apologies I send for times I've made you blue;
Reach out to me with your heart and with your loving hands;
You're the one I'll always love, forever your husband.

A Big Day

Victors today will make speeches tonight;
Only God knows if our favorites are right;
Trying to find the best dog in the fight;
Every year feeling a little less bright.

Trust your best judgment and make yourself heard;
Our Founding Fathers have left us the Word;
Day of decision, we vote our preferred;
And watch our choices get kicked to the curb;
Yesterday's losses are our goals deferred.

A Big Veterans' Day
for Dad

Venerate bravery, raise high your head;
Efforts long made by both living and dead,
Taking on challenges given to them,
Evincing might for the rights of all men;
Ready were they to pay the final price,
And many lives were lost in sacrifice;
Never forget what they have done for you;
Service to all of the red, white, and blue.

Dedicate your thoughts to those of this day,
And think of them when you clasp hands to pray;
Yours is the liberty they fought to gain.

A Big Relief Package

Holiday spirit does not dwell in me;
Ugly, sad season of idiocy;
Merry politicos doling out gifts,
But none for the overtaxed working-class stiffs;
Unto you, Sweet Jesus, all things are saved;
Going to cash in my last IRA.

Starting the layaway sales in September;
Caroling brings in the first of November;
Rush to the mall like a swarm of mad bees,
Only to find you can't find what you need;
Oh, Christmas tree! I don't really want you;
Greenery won't help my sad solitude:
"Elavil now! For a new attitude!"

A Big Night

Carol and Suzie and Barbie and I
Had this night together so many times;
Ready for bed, not asleep until three,
Itching to know what was under the tree.
Suzie and Carol did one year unwrap
Their toys and clothes several days in advance;
Made sure their re-wraps passed Mama's quick glance;
And placed their bad little butts in a trap,
Sad and forlorn as we opened our crap.

Even though this year I probably won't see them,
Very much so they're a part of the reason
Every time I write a poem that is pleasing.

A Big Merry Christmas

Many times these words are heard at this last time of year;
Everyone that says them means them as a means of cheer;
Remember to read between the lines, and you will see
Red and Green are not the reason nor reality;
You must see beyond the Season of Nativity.

Christ was born this day one night two thousand years ago,
His beginnings humble under Heaven's starry glow;
Raised up as a carpenter, his true intent unknown;
In the end, shown as the Christ that history foretold,
Sent by God Our Father to return us to the Fold.
Taught He with His parables His Love of God and Man,
Miracles His witness to His place at God's right hand;
And He knew our weaknesses, and strived to teach us well,
So He lived and died for us to save us from ourselves.

Little Ella

Now we gather one last time;
Even singing Old Lang Syne,
We watch fireballs in the sky.

Young ones jumping in the van;
Ella, don't fall out again;
Asking me to come more near,
Reaches she for my white beard:
"Santa Claus!" she says so dear.

Even though not kin directly,
Very loving she, just three;
"Ella Claus," little Vietnamese.

A Big Old New Year

Children dance in festive costumes,
Happy faces without care;
In the temple, chanting resumes,
Now it floats across night air;
Evening time, passed souls are exhumed
So we know that they're out there,
Each soul needs some grateful prayers.

Next, rice noodles, shoots, and legumes;
Everyone enjoys fine fare,
Waits for fireworks to flare.

Yet to come, two lions dancing,
Eager youths don royal robes;
As drums roll, to kids I'm passing
Red luck money envelopes.

For Practice

Some poems about the trials and tribulations of more than three decades in the private practice of law and my return to writing creatively some ten years ago.

A Big Waste of Time

Probably everything's going to be fine;
Rationalize with the fat bottom line;
Only one day left to finish this task;
Cranium cries out it's too much to ask;
Read one more time this wry poem I've begun,
As lawyering's boring and no longer fun;
Staying on course is just what I can't do;
Terrible failure to work straight on through;
Indecision is not my real excuse,
Nor lack of time do I use as my ruse;
Able to do it if do it I would,
Try to get on it, it better be good;
Oh, God Almighty, I'm under the gun;
Return to writing, one more poem is done.

A Big Pickle

Houston awaits me, and I contemplate:
Early tomorrow my next date with fate;
Ability may not this time avail;
Reality is that they may prevail.
It's the same bell jar I've closed once before;
Now-gone associate messed up the floor;
Going to my knees to clean up once more.

Daunted, I mumble and stare into space,
Asking the one Lord to show me His face;
Yes, I am praying for Amazing Grace.

A Big Extension

Serious look on the good judge's face;
Utters he words that I truly embrace;
Reads me the Riot Act for our report:
"Very deficient, and not of the sort
I'll find acceptable before this Court;
Vary not next time; don't let it fall short."
All that I'd asked for, a chance to revive
Life in this lawsuit I must keep alive.

A Big Disappointment

Assume makes an ass out of you and of me;
Sometimes it's much worse to just let things be;
Seems like some things are so different today;
Only some things in which I had a say.
Can't make a horse drink when it's led to water;
Isn't so hard just to lead lambs to slaughter;
Asking for hard work but never a sample;
Tried to provide a meal ride that was ample,
Even though I set a mournful example.

Going to go back to my solitaire ways;
Only one thing left, to work longer days;
Next time I try to hand off this baton,
Expect I'll be handing it off to my son.

A Big Hole

Slowly sinking into quicksand that's been left to me;
Inkling of disasters that may well yet come to be;
Can I walk alone across this ticking bomb mine field?
Kick my own dumb can for not demanding greater yield.

Adults need their space, so I tried not to interfere;
Too late do I find out there was not much done last year.

Hardly comprehend how long it's been since we were green;
Every chance was given to control one's destiny;
Again I find myself feeling sore, and what's more, betrayed;
Rest not realistic, as my nerves are Torn And Frayed;
Trying still to understand why it must be this way.

A Big College Town

Can't wait to get to the place of my birth,
Only I need just a bit more research;
Long time since I've walked the streets of that city
Under the trees at The State University;
Memories dim since when I was a child;
Born there, not raised, and it's been quite a while;
Underage pre-teen the last time I went;
Saving few dollars, so spare no expense.

Optimum time for this late getaway;
Have depositions, but only one day;
I hope the snow won't be too cold or bleak;
Only am staying there for one short week.

A Big Snore

Deep questions come from the "friendly" examiner;
Exact from the witness a bewildered glance;
Probably expects to be thoroughly hammered;
Obviously cannot catch the nuance;
So, I sit quietly after some banter;
I might take a nap if I have half a chance;
Try paying attention, but it doesn't matter;
I roll my eyes upward when looked at askance;
Only wish the pace would move a bit faster:
Now my crossed leg falls asleep in my pants.

A Bit of Malaise

Writing these lines might seem a waste of time,
Only they keep me of a half-sound mind;
Regret that my wife just cannot understand,
Kindred past spirits are guiding my hand.

High piles of files are still staring me down,
And wonder when I will come back around;
Rimbaud and Roethke and dear Emily
Don't let Death stop them from speaking to me;
Eventually, I'll put more hours to use;
Really, my apathy is no excuse.

A Big Hurry

Loud rings of the telephone
Awaken me in bed at home,
Tell me I'm now past my time;
Empty gas tank comes to mind.

And as I rush down the road,
Gritting teeth and swearing oaths,
Asshole pulls out right in front,
Invites me to smash his trunk:
"Not today, you stupid punk!"

A Big Calling

Gregarious gaffer is calling again;
Obviously thinks I have time to spend;
Doesn't he know just how busy I am?

I don't know when his sad calling will end;
Sometimes he dials up and says he's my friend.

Once I am finished, I might call him back;
Now my desire's to stay right on track.

Let me keep running my meter;
I've got to complete this deal;
Never has money been sweeter;
Everything seems to be real.

Twinge of pain is stabbing my chest;
Wait just a minute, I think it will pass;
Once again over, I'll pass on the tests.

Foibles

Life is just funny sometimes, and no matter what you do, you just can't get out of its way.

A Big Start

Prudishness, you should know, isn't my style,
Except when it comes to some things truly vile;
Really, there's one thing I'd rather not know:
Secrets of ladies' self-created glows;
Only last night while I watched the T.V.,
New woman's product was revealed to me:
A thin buzzer worn on her small fingertip,
Lightly applied to her soft nether lips.

Matrons regaled its thrills in a full lobby
As if they had never had such a fun hobby;
Silently overheard by an old bat,
Smiling affirmance, she knew about that,
And then the bombshell that mightily blew:
Grandmother told the girls she has one, too!
Explain to me why the company Trojan
Raucously broadcasts that old girl's implosions.

A Big Change

Angst I'm feeling once again,
Now that my head's shaggy;
Never want my look to end,
Unless it bothers me;
Ask myself why do I bend,
Lurch toward conformity.

Have to sit still and be tough,
Although that won't protect
Itchy little clumps of fluff from
Rolling down my neck;
Cannot stand this aggravation;
Underneath chafe in frustration;
Terrible abomination.

A Big Meal

Maybe buffet is the way your egg rolls;
Asian cuisine, I say, "Best made at home."
Pork bits and bean curd in red pepper gravy
Offers a dish that's both healthy and savory;
Hungry big kids at the table go crazy.

Take a nice portion and put it on rice;
Only need chopsticks, perhaps some more spice;
Family recipe hundreds of years;
Undulate later when it burns your rear.

A Butacci Fibonacci

Bring

Us

The best

Alfredo,

Chianti vino,

Cioppino with mussels and clams,

Italian hot cross buns in a nice red-cloth basket.

A Big Number

Fearsome day of myth and lore;
Ripe red tide of blood and gore;
Ides of March since days of yore;
Death spree in unholy war;
Always ghastly on the screen;
Yet, your eyes watch every scene.

Today is the day of dread;
Have to hold on to your head,
Else you might find yourself dead.

Try not to succumb to it;
Hell's no place to wait and sit;
It's no matter anyway,
Reaper comes this day your way;
Terrified, you clench your teeth,
Ever the remote in reach;
Even though you just might scream,
Never change Channel 13!
Try to sleep scared in your bed,
Horror image fills your head.

High Neighbor

Destroyer of body that conquers the mind;
Ever so present, never behind;
Viceroy of vices since old ancient times;
Insider trader of health in decline;
Languish in anguish with the tie that binds.

Wink at the mirror with an eye so blind;
Hapless pretender is what you will find;
Indulgence from those that think themselves kind
Serves you quite well with their, "Well, never mind."
Kill yourself off while you're killing off time;
Even to Death you would sadly resign;
You'd find him waiting with impatient whines.

A Big Obsession

Only those golfers among us will know,
Balls of white, dimpled, set our hearts a'glow;
Stand we on tee boxes, taking dead aim;
Every round different, oftentimes strange;
Suffer we fools so obsessed with this game!
Savoring good shots, lamenting the bad;
Ignorant of the good time we just had;
Onward our conquest, our pursuit of par;
Never revealing what our true scores are.

A Big Remembrance

Rainy reverie this morning takes me back in time;
Every dripping raincoat forming puddles in a line;
Mister Funchess walking down the hall with his broad stick;
Each of us goes quiet, you can hear the wall clock tick;
Michael Brannon now the one about to get a lick;
Brace yourself against the sink, and pray that it comes quick.
Ripples of girls' titters flowing up and down the hall;
All of us just waiting for it, both the big and small;
Now we hear a loud "boom" which reverberates so deep;
Comes back Michael Brannon, a stout lad that doesn't weep;
Everyone is guessing that he turned the other cheek.

A Big Reversal

Have never known such transactions before,
As my sons give me shirts they'll wear no more;
Nephews have left me some collared Tees, too,
Dunned from their jobs at the Country Club pool.

Maybe they're out of style, not that I care;
Each one is raiment that gladly I'll wear.

Underwear isn't a part of this deal;
Pants long and too tight, I'm not that surreal;
Sad, I find these shirts reflect what I feel.

Comes the Day

Sometimes, an unforeseen triumph occurs;
August's last dog days now seem like a blur;
Isn't it funny how time slips away?
Never did think I would live 'til today;
Try now to find a new reason to pray,
Since there's one thing less to turn my hair gray.

Winter takes respite from her harshest freeze;
Insects and birds chirp in spring-like cool breeze;
Never a time when I've been half this pleased.

Terrible struggles for decades are gone;
Hiding our faces, not having much fun;
Exclaiming yearly next year is the one.

So, today is our own day in the sun,
Understanding what it is to be one;
Patience rewarded to those who kept faith;
Example of what one does with God's grace;
Realization that He has kept pace.

Bring on new challenges, show us the way;
Our day is here, none can take it away;
Winners descend from their mountain of toil;
Losers no more, this our permanent spoil.

A Big Hand

Trying to retain my gin rummy crown;
Her face is smiling, while mine holds a frown;
Endgame approaching, and I'm going down.

Cards have betrayed me again and again;
How can I win with four aces her friends?
Able to make some small points here and there;
Might I pick up the pile? Better beware;
Plenty of points down there staring at me;
Even my luck will change eventually;
Exigencies force me to a bolder turn;
Now she has gone out, and how I've been burned.

Lust Never Sleeps

Longing beginning in one's early years;
Understand later it won't disappear;
Sexual organ that grows in one's head;
Trying desire for someone to bed.

None can control it, and few can suppress;
External forces cause internal stress;
Various manifestations, one theme;
Even will follow one into one's dreams, but
Reality isn't quite what one sees.

Seems like advancing years would this abate:
Last thought before sleep, first thought when awake;
Exacerbated by media forms;
Even a new industry was thus born;
Perhaps pure wretchedness, perhaps a norm;
Suffer it silently, or write a poem.

Of Pens and Poets

Most editors, myself included, disfavor poems about the writing process; perhaps they strike too close to home?

A Big Acrostic Challenge

Powerful tool in the hands of a few;
Open some eyes, let them see things anew;
Expressive feelings, heart-felt point of view;
Timorous squeaks from the turns of a screw;
Rigorous vision the whole cold night through;
Yesternight's blackness tomorrow's soft blues.

Pleasance of mind is what he hopes you'll find;
Opens his soul in the hope folks are kind;
Eyes of the dreamer transcend sense of time;
Message received by those who have like minds.

Original thoughts that just cannot be taught;
Rejections hurt him when his thoughts aren't bought.

Pray for the soul of the miserable scribe;
Open self-loathing and subject to jibes;
Every day keeping his faint hopes alive;
Trying to send you some interesting vibes.

A Big Pity

Pity the poor man who chose as his lot
Over and over to snow us with rot;
Ever so fain to relate his vain thoughts;
Tries to explain what he knows God has wrought.

Leader of nations, a nation of one;
After each ration, a new one begun;
Rhythmic riddles in hopes of a pun;
Idiosyncrasies he thinks are fun;
Asking for laurels that he has not won;
Testing our patience, our time his to dun.

A Big Rejection

"Really, you shouldn't have wasted our time;
Emasculate rhymes you tried so hard to find;
Jokes of your timbre we can't find sublime;
Even, admitted, there were some good lines;
Chuckles did utter, not worthy of mind;
Totally folksy with vision so blind;
Idiot savant, we will not be kind;
Onerous burden to us you assigned,
Nowhere Man maladies your silly grind."

LED dial on my radio clock
Every night asks me what I think I've got;
Try to remember those lessons well-taught;
Triumph denied due to what I am not;
Eventually, maybe, I will get across;
Ready to bare it until life is lost.

A Big Superego

Misery seeps through Poor Pitiful Me:
Is this all of life there is going to be?
Shout or just cry out from the tallest tree;
Timber will tumble and bring death to thee.
Everyone's hustling, all in a groove;
Really, there's no place that I wouldn't move.

Legend of his own mocking brand;
Aged fabrications with a single hand;
Maker of bread for the masses;
Bringer of rhymes to the kind;
Rings on four fingers that reach for the clapper,
Everyman's stylistic natural disaster,
Mentor host to the mostly blind;
Only wastes what thoughts he can find;
Never-amounted-to-anything bastard;
Terrible child in a terrible time.

A Big Blank

Whether 'tis noble,
Right or wrong,
It is your lot
To play your song;
Ever your hands
Reach for the notes, yet
Silence results,

But you press on, and
Look with unease;
Only today you
Can't find the
Keys.

A Cross Dick

Finding nothing to say today,
Upset at responses that come my way;
Could it be time to shut this thing down?
King of glib rhymery wears a fool's crown.

Idyllic dribblings from a misfit;
Truly, there's no one that gives a big shit.

A Big Adviser

Just when I feel I have nothing to say,
Under The Weight of a new poem each day;
Son Johnny sends an apt message my way:
Try to Get Back to Things We Said Today.

"Really, book poetry's not your best style,
Even though I like it once in a while;
Lessen the rhyming verticality;
Acrostics are not what I prefer to see;
Xerox more memories to send to me."

A Big Announcement

Although it pains me to say this to you,
Now is the time; I must tell you the truth;
Not every day will there be poems du jour;
Of course, you know why, you've been on the tour.
Unfortunate how my time has gone south;
Need to make more money running my mouth;
Certainly you'll see some more poems from me;
Exactly when? Que sera, that we'll see;
Maybe it's better to do it this way;
Every day is but just Another Day;
Never would I give you mere quantity,
Try now to send you some real quality.

On the Launch of the Glass Coin

Today you launch on a new sea your literary ship,
Hardy and so capable of moving pun and quip,
Ever ready to salvo head shots gunned from the hip.

Gazing through the clear boat bottom, you will see the deep;
Looking to the sky, you'll find a cloud whose face you'll keep;
All are one, but some fine lines define the ones in twos;
Strands of hope afloat on this boat, your course we know true,
Setting sail in such a way to make you see things through.

Cheers to you, dear captains, may your voyage take you far;
Only time will tell if you will hitch onto a star;
In the meantime, try to keep the poets from the bar;
Next you know, they'll stumble, and mumble out a "Yar!"

Reply

to Nicole in Eugene

Regarding your rude e-mail sent me today,
Evincing your disdain for mine sent your way;
May I remind you of one single fact?
Only last month you sent me one with tact,
Very sincere in your poetry submission,
Eager to be part of our first edition.

Do know that I read your poems in due course;
Even though I said no, I've seen much worse;
Letting you down was not my true intention;
Editors vary in style and convention;
Try to learn from this, as you should know better:
Everyone gets their own rejection letters.

Until you learn this, your path will be hard,
Not likely to turn from a scribe to a bard;
Successful poems are just what you should read,
Unless you think you have all that you need;
Better to learn from those that have endured,
Sharing politeness in letters and words;
Chances are greater that you will be heard.
Refusing gifts of verse surely your right
If you wish never to expand your sight,
But being mean-spirited only hurts you,
Except when it hurts your poor editor, too.

A Big Etheree

By
Inking
Garrulous

Experiments,
Trying on new hats,
Harboring delusions,
Eking out my eager lines,
Righteously, I made your mind mine.
Ever my words I send to you free,
Even have made you a big etheree.

Of Body and Soul

Growing older and getting old is quite the drag, but realistically speaking, what is the alternative?

A Big Appetite

Gorge yourself like a mad bull in full rage;
Lessen your chances of reaching old age;
Upset your stomach and block your blood vessels
'Til you are all flab and lacking in muscles;
Tell yourself one more time diets can wait,
Only to find out one day it's too late;
Near to exploding, with death at your door;
Yet, you have room for just one big meal more.

A Big Space Invader

Underneath the porous skin of us all
Lie little things that we cannot see;
Trying to hide out like mice in a wall,
Residing inside us for free.
An apparatus' soft inner call can
Send out a signal to read,
Ovaries, mammaries, testicles all
Understand why this must be:
Not only tragedies cause us to fall,
Death sometimes comes naturally.

A Big Discomfort

Can't understand why it is this must be;
You have to slide your thing deep into me;
Steady your hand as you enter my sex;
Try to be careful and follow the text;
Only imagine what's going in next;
Shivers my timber, it cries in reflex.
Can you please hurry, you're hurting my wood;
Oh, say, can you see anything that's not good?
Probably this will be the only time
Ever that we will be thusly entwined.

A Big Blocker

Counting your calories won't bring it down;
Having to do without, What A Bringdown;
One thing you have to do every day:
Live your Lush Life in a healthier way;
Eating what you are is not what to do:
Start eating vegetables and more fresh fruit!
Try hard to exercise, 'though it's no fun;
Even then your battle will not be won:
Reach for the bottle that holds the smart pills;
Only imbibe some occasional swills;
Lessen your chances of clogs that can kill.

A Big Super-Hero

Crusher of Evil Lipidites!
Reach into my mauled tissues;
Energize my Steel Pulse to fight;
Save me from "serious issues";
Take my life blood and make it right;
Oils seep deep through my fissures;
Restore me through thy strength and might!

A Big Task

Suffer yourself all the things that you like;
Treat yourself better with things that are right;
Anxious beginning to this the new year;
Rich is my harvest, but flat is my beer;
To not to be is the thing we all fear;
Inverted portions of what we hold dear
Now I will take in without any cheer;
Goodness resulting, but not without tears.

Apples, they say, keep the doctor away;

Doctor appointments too frequent these days;
I don't mind going, but I'd like a say;
Exiting strategy: be old and gray;
Try hard to keep the grim reaper away.

A Big Concern

Clean bill of health you just got for yourself,
And now you're worried for somebody else;
Not some old person that you've never known,
Could be a close friend with whom you have grown;
Ever you pray that things will turn out right;
Realize that there's some things you can't fight.

Medical doctors will have to perform,
Ascertain if something's out of the norm;
You sit by idly and wait for the news;
Best to be patient, they take several views;
Examinations no one can refuse.

A Big Pill

Lozenge of supposed relief
Only brought her woe and grief;
Red-rimmed eyes that told the tale;
Terrible vision, past the pale;
Almost breaking, near hysteria,
Because the Hot Dog Woman cut Sarah.

A Big Mass

In bed I lie in morning time,
Not knowing why I stay;
Eventually, in bed I'll die;
Rash hopes do lie that way.
Try not to think what awaits;
Instead, I cast my wind to fate:
Although it's late, there's time to waste.

A Big Antenna

A big anachronism stands tall from my back yard patio,
Never activated 'cause My Sweet Lord told me so:
"Try, child, to seek out things that are beyond iron's reach;
Everness goes through me, and no tower fills that breach;
Never will a wave-length from the blue skies high above
Nearly duplicate the warmth that is Our Father's love;
Always keep Us in your mind; keep searching for the Dove."

A Big Lift

Rastaman Vibration drifts my way;
Ever-living sound all the way from JA;
Gently soothes me on this trying day;
Grooves so rooted in a song of praise;
Ask myself why I don't play it all day;
Exorcise my soul while my brain's in disarray.

Messages abound in what they play;
Understand the meanings in what they say:
Send Greetings to the Father each and every day;
It's not necessary to go to church to pray:
Chant Down Babylon on your own today.

A Big Send-Off

Can't say you're going away by yourself;
Residue's left from the one just before;
Even a bit of you still on the shelf;
Maybe together you'll find Heaven's door;
Always, they say, there is room for one more.
Time-tested method beyond any grave;
It will do nothing to immortal soul;
One only chooses it if one is brave;
Not to my liking, please send me home whole.

A Big Time

Fearful that life's but a sad mystery?
Only some find blessed sweet harmony.
Riding on rough tides, it seems, every day?
Even in bad times, have good things to say.
Verify that you are one of a whole,
Even though each plays a small solo role;
Rest your head gently, your soul can't be sold.

About the Author

John Lambremont, Sr. is a poet and writer from Baton Rouge, Louisiana, U.S.A., and was the editor of *Big River Poetry Review*. John's poems have been published internationally in many reviews and anthologies, including *Pacific Review, Clarion, The Minetta Review, Flint Hills Review*, and *Taj Mahal Review*, and he has been nominated for The Pushcart Prize. John's poetry volumes include *Dispelling The Indigo Dream* (Local Gems Poetry Press 2013); *What It Means To Be A Man (And Other Poems Of Life And Death)* (Finishing Line Press 2014); *The Moment Of Capture* (Lit Fest Press 2017); and *Old Blues, New Blues*, (Pski's Porch Publishing 2018).

Acknowledgments

A number of poems included in this book have appeared previously in the following:

'A Big Lady', 'A Big Pioneer', 'A Big Icon', 'A Big Star', 'A Big Clown', 'A Big Mind', 'A Big Vision', 'A Big Red X', 'A Big Icon', 'A Big Old-Timer', 'A Big Iconoclast', and 'A Big Significant Other' in *Jerry Jazz Musician*

'A Far Cry' in *The Ampersand Review*

'Black-Eyed Susans' and 'Ephemeron' in *Cantos*

'A Big Dalliance' in *Suisin Valley Review*

'Red On Green' and 'At Sundown' in *Luney Writers Anthology, Volume 1* (Literary Lunes)

'The Caretaker' in *Greensilk Journal*

'A Late Breakthrough' in *Flutter Poetry Journal*

'Football Hero 1967' in *Acreage*

'Quality People Wanted' in *Retail Woes* (Local Gems Poetry Press)

'Major Thoroughfare' appeared previously in *partyof1.net*

'Eddie Anderson' appeared previously in *The Baton Rouge Lawyer*

'A Big Fibonacci' appeared previously in *The Fib Review*

'High Neighbor' and 'A Big Apprehension' appeared previously in *The Stray Branch*

'A Big Anniversary' and 'To My Other Mother' appeared previously in *Cupid's Arrow* (Creative Talents Unleashed)

'A Big Acrostic Challenge' appeared previously in *Bell's Letters Poet*

'Reply' appeared previously in *Blood On The Floor: How Writers Survive Rejection* (Cairn Press)

'Lust Never Sleeps' appeared previously in *Lust 7 Deadly Sins Vol .1* (Pure Slush Books)

'A Big Time' appeared previously in *Essential Existentialism* (Creative Talents Unleashed)

Also from TRUTH SERUM PRESS

https://truthserumpress.net/catalogue/

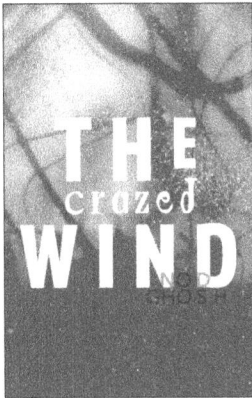

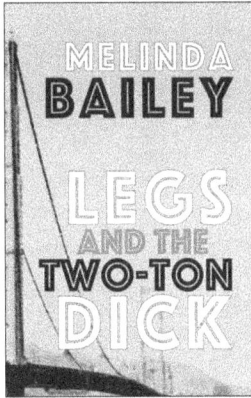

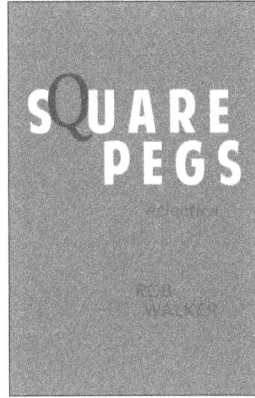

- *The Crazed Wind* by Nod Ghosh
  978-1-925536-58-4 (paperback) 978-1-925536-59-1 (eBook)
- *Legs and the Two-Ton Dick* by Melinda Bailey
  978-1-925536-37-9 (paperback) 978-1-925536-38-6 (eBook)
- *Square Pegs* by Rob Walker
  978-1-925536-62-1 (paperback) 978-1-925536-63-8 (eBook)

- *Cheat Sheets* by Edward O'Dwyer
  978-1-925536-60-7 (paperback) 978-1-925536-61-4 (eBook)
- *Kiss Kiss* by Paul Beckman
  978-1-925536-21-8 (paperback) 978-1-925536-22-5 (eBook)
- *Dollhouse Masquerade* by Samuel E. Cole
  978-1-925536-43-0 (paperback) 978-1-925536-44-7 (eBook)

Also from TRUTH SERUM PRESS

https://truthserumpress.net/catalogue/

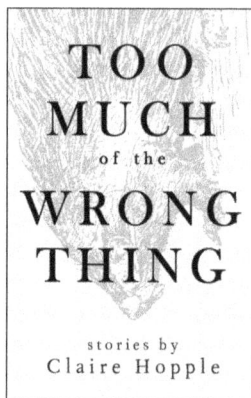

- *On the Bitch* by Matt Potter
  978-1-925536-45-4 (paperback) 978-1-925536-46-1 (eBook)
- *Inklings* by Irene Buckler
  978-1-925536-41-6 (paperback) 978-1-925536-42-3 (eBook)
- *Too Much of the Wrong Thing* by Claire Hopple
  978-1-925536-33-1 (paperback) 978-1-925536-34-8 (eBook)

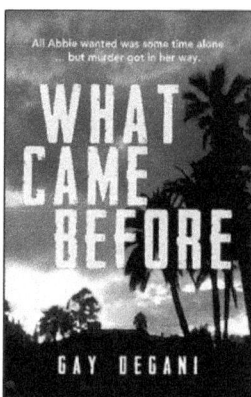

- *Track Tales* by Mercedes Webb-Pullman
  978-1-925536-35-5 (paperback) 978-1-925536-36-2 (eBook)
- *True Truth Serum Vol. #1*
  978-1-925536-29-4 (paperback) 978-1-925536-30-0 (eBook)
- *What Came Before* by Gay Degani
  978-1-925536-05-8 (paperback) 978-1-925536-06-5 (eBook)

Also from TRUTH SERUM PRESS

https://truthserumpress.net/catalogue/

- *Hello Berlin!* by Jason S. Andrews
  978-1-925536-11-9 (paperback) 978-1-925536-12-6 (eBook)
- *Deer Michigan* by Jack C. Buck
  978-1-925536-25-6 (paperback) 978-1-925536-26-3 (eBook)
- *Rain Check* by Levi Andrew Noe
  978-1-925536-09-6 (paperback) 978-1-925536-10-2 (eBook)

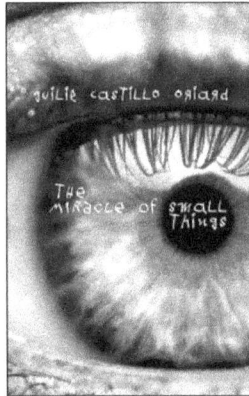

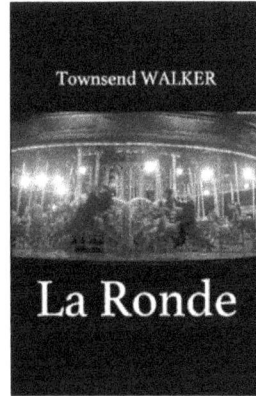

- *Luck and Other Truths* by Richard Mark Glover
  978-1-925101-77-5 (paperback) 978-1-925536-04-1 (eBook)
- *The Miracle of Small Things* by Guilie Castillo Oriard
  978-1-925101-73-7 (paperback) 978-1-925101-74-4 (eBook)
- *La Ronde* by Townsend Walker
  978-1-925101-64-5 (paperback) 978-1-925101-65-2 (eBook